STUDY GUIDE AND WORKBOOK

THE MYSTERY OF THE NATIVITY
AN INSPIRATIONAL DRAMA
ON THE NATIVITY OF JESUS CHRIST

CLAUDETTE FRANCIS

authorHOUSE®

AuthorHouse™
1663 Liberty Drive
Bloomington, IN 47403
www.authorhouse.com
Phone: 833-262-8899

Published by AuthorHouse   10/14/2022

ISBN: 978-1-4817-2731-0 (sc)
ISBN: 978-1-4817-2741-9 (e)

"The Scripture quotations contained herein are from the New Revised Standard Version Bible: Catholic Edition copyright © 1993 and 1989 by the Division of Christian Education of the National Council of the Churches of Christ in the U.S.A." Used by permission. All rights reserved."

Print information available on the last page.

Any people depicted in stock imagery provided by Thinkstock are models, and such images are being used for illustrative purposes only. Certain stock imagery © Thinkstock.

This book is printed on acid-free paper.

Because of the dynamic nature of the Internet, any web addresses or links contained in this book may have changed since publication and may no longer be valid. The views expressed in this work are solely those of the author and do not necessarily reflect the views of the publisher, and the publisher hereby disclaims any responsibility for them.

Claudette Francis
4 Sergio Marchi Street
Toronto, Ontario, Canada
M3L OB6
PH: 647 828 3376
Email:swancletus28@gmail.com

TABLE OF CONTENTS

ACKNOWLEDGEMENT

Grateful thanks are extended to Fran Richardson, MED DIM MTS, who after reading my book—*THE MYSTERY OF THE RESURRECTION*[1] sought my permission to develop a STUDY GUIDE & WORKBOOK to accompany the text.

With great insight, and knowledge of the Word of God, she put her God-given talents and her time to work, and so brought to fruition an inspiring Study Guide/Workbook. Richardson refers to her work in the following terms: "An excellent teaching tool for use with new Christians or for revitalizing the spirit of those who know the story well."

Richardson has also given me a prototype for my current book—*THE MYSTERY OF THE NATIVITY*[2]. Patterned after her book, I have now developed a Study Guide/Workbook for this second drama THE MYSTERY OF THE NATIVITY. This will remain the pattern for all of my future dramas of this nature.

She continues to work in her Anglican Community, teaching Theological Education.

1   Francis, C. *The Mystery of the Resurrection* 4th edition, Authorhouse, Bloomington, 2008

2.   Francis, C. *The Mystery of the Nativity* Authorhouse, Bloomington, 2012

INTRODUCTION

Welcome to *The Mystery of the Nativity*, a play, a Bible Study and a reflection exercise. This workbook is designed to be a companion to the book *The Mystery of the Nativity* by Claudette Francis. You may choose to use this workbook by yourself or in a group. Either way, we trust that you will find both the book and the exercise welcome additions to your personal devotions.

Why Study the Nativity of Jesus?

From the time Adam and Eve acted in spiritual blindness and committed the first sin, the sin of disobedience, God, promised to send a Savior to redeem mankind and bring them back to him. The LORD GOD said to the serpent . . .

I will put enmity between you and the woman, and between your offspring and hers: he will strike your head, and you will strike his heel.' (Genesis 3: 15)

The Nativity of Jesus is the fulfillment of this promise that God made to mankind in the Garden of Eden.

Why a Play?

The Mystery of The Nativity is written in the form of a play, one that can be read or one that can be enacted. By participating in the play, there is an opportunity to get into the story, to be more

INTRODUCTION

than a bystander, looking in. The story becomes real. God speaks to us through one another, and so God may speak to us through the characters in the play.

Additional Items You will Need

In addition to the Mystery of the Nativity and this workbook, you will require a pen, a highlighter, a pad of small sticky notes or flags, extra writing paper, and at least two different translations of the Bible. Alternate translations may assist you in understanding specific biblical verses.

GETTING STARTED

For maximum benefit, quickly read through *The Mystery of the Nativity* in one sitting, then continue with the workbook.

REFLECTION

Reflecting on what you have just read, write down your thoughts and feelings. (Because these are your thoughts and feelings, there are no right or wrong answers.)

When I read the book I thought:

_____

_____

_____

_____

_____

_____

_____

_____

_____

_____

_____

_____

_____

REFLECTION

When I read the book I felt:

_____

_____

_____

_____

_____

_____

_____

_____

_____

_____

_____

Scene 1

The trial begins. The prosecutor reads the charges. Who is being charged, and what are the charges?

_____
_____
_____
_____
_____
_____
_____
_____
_____
_____
_____
_____
_____

How did King Herod first learn about the child born to be King of the Jews? Describe his reaction to the news?

_____
_____
_____
_____

_____

_____

_____

_____

_____

_____

_____

_____

Speculate on what you think King Herod would have done if indeed he had the opportunity to visit and see the Child in Bethlehem?

_____

_____

_____

_____

_____

_____

_____

_____

_____

_____

_____

_____

The Bible (OLD TESTAMENT, the past NEW TESTAMENT, the present and REVELATION, the future) is all about one central figure—Jesus Christ the Son of God. In the OLD TESTAMENT God raised up prophets to tell the people that a Messiah will come to redeem them from their sins. His promise was fulfilled in the NEW TESTAMENT. What is to come is foretold in Revelation.

Read: Genesis 3:15, Isaiah 7:14, Matthew 1:23

Scene 2

Who is the woman referred to in Genesis 3:15? Is she the same woman referred to in Isaiah 7:14 and Matthew 1: 23?

How was this prophesy fulfilled?

_____

_____

_____

_____

_____

_____

_____

_____

_____

_____

Read: Luke 1: 27

Explain what is meant by 'the house of David.'

_____

_____

_____

_____

_____

_____

_____

_____

_____

_____

_____

_____

_____

Read: Luke 2: 8-20

Scene 3

Luke is the only one to make mention of the Shepherds.

At the time of Jesus' birth there were many different people living in Israel . . . there were priests, scribes, doctors, King, governor, Romans, Greeks, but the angel of the Lord did not announce the Good News to any of them.

Who were the first people to hear these words? I am bringing you good news of great joy for all the people: to you is born this day in the city of David a Savior who is the Messiah, the Lord. This will be a sign to you: you will find a child wrapped in bands of cloth and lying in a manger.

_____

_____

_____

_____

_____

_____

_____

_____

_____

_____

_____

_____

Why do you think the Author made Shepherd Ess one of her characters? Give the name of one shepherdess in the Bible.

_____

_____

_____

_____

_____

_____

_____

_____

_____

_____

_____

_____

_____

Read: Luke 2:12; Luke 23: 52

Do you see similarities in these two passages? What are they?

_____

_____

_____

_____

_____

Read: Matthew 1:18-25, 2: 13-15

Scenes 4 & 5

Define "predicament." What was Joseph's predicament? Relate how he handled his predicament?

_____

_____

_____

_____

_____

_____

_____

_____

_____

_____

_____

After reading the above passages, what conclusion did you come to regarding Joseph's character and personality?

_____

_____

_____

_____

_____

_____

_____

_____

_____

_____

_____

_____

_____

Read: Matthew 1: 18-25

Joseph wanted to break off his engagement to Mary. What was his reason for wanting to do so?

How did Joseph learn that Mary was chosen to be the mother of a son from the Holy Spirit? How did Joseph respond to the dream? What name did Joseph give Mary's son? What was Jesus' mission on earth?

_____

_____

_____

_____

_____

_____

_____

_____

_____

_____

_____

_____

_____

Read: Isaiah7:14

Jewish maidens were aware of God's promise that a maiden is with child and would bring forth the Messiah, so it was obvious that that task could be given to any Jewish maiden yet when the news was announced to Mary a Jewish maiden, she was perplexed. Why was she perplexed at what the Angel told her?

_____

_____

_____

_____

_____

_____

_____

_____

_____

_____

_____

Read Luke 1: 39-40

Which of the three virtues—faith, hope, and love—do you think Mary exercised when she went with haste to visit Elizabeth? Give a reason for your choice.

_____

_____

_____

_____

_____

_____

_____

_____

_____

_____

Read: Matthew 2: 16-19

Mary treasured all these words and pondered them in her heart. What words did she ponder in her heart? How do you suppose she felt being at the centre of this event?

_____

_____

_____

_____

_____

_____

_____

_____

_____

_____

_____

_____

Read: Matthew 2:13-15

What was Joseph's response to the angel's command to take the child and his mother and flee to Egypt, and remain there until I tell you; for Herod is about to search for the child, to destroy him?

_____

_____

_____

_____

_____

_____

_____

_____

_____

_____

The Ruler from Bethlehem

But you, O Bethlehem of Ephrathah, who are one of the little clans of Judah, from you shall come forth for me one who is to rule in Israel, whose origin is from of old, from ancient days. (Micah 5:2)

Read: Luke 2: 1-7

Scene 6

Joseph and Mary lived in Galilee. Explain how God's word was fulfilled that His Son Jesus would be born in Bethlehem and not in Nazareth, Galilee.

_____

_____

_____

_____

_____

_____

_____

_____

_____

_____

_____

_____

_____

Why were Mary and Joseph turned away from the inn?

_____

_____

_____

_____

_____

_____

_____

_____

_____

In this drama the Innkeeper was portrayed as an opportunist. Give reasons for this view point.

_____

_____

_____

_____

_____

_____

_____

_____

_____

_____

_____

Read: Luke 2: 25-35

Scene 7

Who was Simeon, and where did he live?

What was his role in the nativity story?

_____

_____

_____

_____

_____

_____

_____

_____

_____

_____

_____

Read: Luke 2:27

How was Simeon able to recognize the child as the one revealed to him by the Holy Spirit?

_____

_____

_____

_____

_____

_____

_____

_____

_____

_____

_____

_____

_____

_____

Who said these words: "This child is destined for the falling and the rising of many in Israel, and to be a sign that will be opposed so that the inner thoughts of many will be revealed?" Explain the meaning of this prophecy.

_____

_____

_____

_____

_____

_____

_____

_____

_____

_____

_____

_____

_____

_____
_____

Simeon prophesied that someone's heart would be pierced by a sword. Was this prophesy actually fulfilled? Explain.

_____
_____
_____
_____
_____
_____
_____
_____
_____
_____
_____
_____

Read: Luke 2: 36-38

Who was Anna, and what part did she play in the Nativity story?

_____
_____
_____

End-time Prophesy.

A multitude of camels shall cover you,

The young camels of Midian and Ephah; all those from Sheba shall come. They shall bring gold and frankincense, and shall proclaim the praise of the LORD. (Isaiah 60:6)

Read Matthew 2:9-12

Scene 8

Do you see any differences between the 'End time Prophesy' and the passage taken from Matthew's Gospel?

_____

_____

_____

_____

_____

_____

_____

_____

_____

_____

_____

Matthew was the only one to mention the Visit of the Wise Men. Did the wise men visit the Baby Jesus in the manger? Which verses dispute this long standing tradition? Can you explain why tradition figures out that there were only three wise men?

How old was Jesus when the wise men saw him? What statement in this scene helped you conclude that Jesus was not a baby when the wise men arrived at his parents' house?

_____

_____

_____

_____

_____

_____

_____

_____

_____

_____

_____

_____

_____

_____

The Massacre of the Infants

A voice is heard in Ramah, lamentation and bitter weeping. Rachel is weeping for her children; she refused to be comforted for her children, because they are no more. (Jeremiah 31: 15)

Read: Matthew 2: 16-18

Scene 9

Jeremiah's prophecy was fulfilled in the New Testament. Give details of when and how this prophecy was fulfilled.

_____

_____

_____

_____

_____

_____

_____

_____

_____

_____

_____

_____

_____

Matthew was the only one to mention the Massacre of the infants. Did the reading of this Scene help you to understand what the mothers suffered? How strong was the mothers' case against King Herod? Give reasons for your answers.

_____
_____
_____
_____
_____
_____
_____
_____
_____
_____
_____

Compare and contrast the characters of Judge Deborah and the Prosecutor Madam Louisburg in this Scene.

_____
_____
_____
_____
_____
_____

_____

_____

_____

_____

_____

_____

_____

Did this trial do anything to alleviate the suffering the mothers underwent on that dreadful day when King Herod ordered the massacre of the infants? Explain.

_____

_____

_____

_____

_____

_____

_____

_____

_____

_____

_____

_____

_____

Scenes 10 & 11

Were you expecting the jury to convict King Herod on all four counts? Why or Why not?

_____

_____

_____

_____

_____

_____

_____

_____

_____

_____

_____

_____

_____

Describe Herod's reaction to the guilty verdict? Do you think he had a fair trial? Comment on the sentence meted out to King Herod.

_____

_____

_____

_____

_____

_____

_____

_____

_____

_____

_____

_____

_____

Reading this story as a court trial, what impact did it have on you in its contemporary form?

_____

_____

_____

_____

_____

_____

_____

_____

_____

_____

_____

_____

Scenes 12 & Conclusion

Read: Mark 12: 28-31, John 13:34-35

Describe the New Commandment of love that Jesus gave us. What is the difference between the First Commandment of love, mentioned in Mark 12: 28-31 and the New Commandment of love mentioned in John 13: 34-35?

In what ways do you practice the New Commandment of Love?

_____

_____

_____

_____

_____

_____

_____

_____

_____

_____

_____

_____

_____

Read: Philippians 2:6-8

What does Jesus mean by these words: "I divested myself of my Godhead, taking the form of a slave, being born in human likeness?"

_____

_____

_____

_____

_____

_____

_____

_____

_____

_____

_____

_____

Did the men and women in this drama contribute to your understanding of the Nativity of Jesus and the events that took place in Israel some two thousand years ago?

_____

_____

_____

_____

_____

_____

_____

_____

_____

_____

_____

Write down in your own words what you consider to
be the most significant part of the Mystery of the
Nativity.

Who is your favorite character? Give reasons for
your answer.

_____

_____

_____

_____

_____

_____

_____

_____

_____

_____

_____

_____

The Mystery of the Nativity enables others to hear the story of the birth of Jesus in a contemporary format. May this exercise have assisted you in understanding the reality of the birth of Jesus-, the Messiah, Savior and Redeemer of the world.

~

Printed in the United States
by Baker & Taylor Publisher Services